Los Angeles Dreams

Rich Hebron

Los Angeles Dreams

Rich Hebron

Books by Rich Hebron

Homeless but Human
Primary Ponderings

Nuance & Notes Series

Chicago Clarity
Paris Beauty
New York Energy
Los Angeles Dreams
Miami Magic
Milwaukee Sensibility
Mexico City Merriness
London Happening

Written by Rich Hebron
Illustrated by Kenneth Ferguson

Milly Moves to the Farm
The Boy and the Rocketship

Rich Edition Classics

The Great Gatsby

Rich Hebron is an American author. He has lived half his life in Chicago and the other half on a farm in rural Wisconsin. He fuses these backgrounds together to draw inspiration and live a meaningful life in a world accelerated by the internet and digital technology. He hosts the Rich Conversations Podcast where he explores self-development and talks with friends in art and science fields.

Connect with Rich: @richhebron

For those who want to pursue their dreams

Author's Note

My first near-death experience happened on the farm. An oil line blew on the tractor and became engulfed in flames. I jumped from it. My second near-death experience occurred four years afterwards. This time, three men pointed Uzi guns at my face, threatening to shoot me. Fortunately, it was just another reminder that life will end—all our lives. So how do we want ours to be?

After initially going fast, with the adrenaline from the encounter lasting months, I decided to stop. The difference between speed and velocity is that velocity is speed in a direction. Anyone can go fast—especially in circles. But it takes skill and something deeper to channel energy with purpose. Refining purpose requires restarting at the beginning. Be open and see what's happening. Pursue curiosity and, above all, patience.

My curiosity led me to hotel lobbies. I spent time visiting different ones in downtown Chicago and just sat, observed, and wrote notes, often sipping espresso or red wine. An appreciation for details developed. Gratitude followed. Every thing was there for a reason. Nothing was a coincidence. The creators of the spaces aimed to evoke particular emotions and feelings in people. They staged a vibe.

I learned that design affects our mind and influences our culture. The whole of something is the result of individual things. From a pencil to a house. From a shoe to our cities. From a light fixture to our lives. The story of our life is the result of every individual decision we make. The universe is the result of every individual atom.

Beauty is the result of those small, individual components. Love is understanding those small, individual components.

My passion and appreciation for detail expanded from hotel lobbies to virtually everything in life and in people. But something I especially had fun with was observing the designs on building facades. My favorites were those resembling nature. They possessed the character I aspire to be: dynamic, flexible, playful, and fruitful. Things that are alive are adaptable. Things that are dead are stiff, rigid, and brittle. Since human beings are part of nature, the same is true for people and their ideas and perspectives.

I encourage you to reflect on the follow questions:

- *Are current environments failing to design nuance?*
- *If design affects culture, what are the ramifications of prioritizing cheap and fast?*
- *Is a society that ignores patience a healthy one?*
- *If individuality is abandoned, is Love too?*

This is a series called *Nuance & Notes*.
This is a book of nuance of Los Angeles with notes from my mind and observations in the world.

A person doesn't have to spend much time in Los Angeles before they think: "I get it. I get why people live here." Los Angeles is enchanting. A fresh and hopeful aura perfumes the air. It's enormous in size as well as ambition. It contains every weather, scenery, and skillset. More than any other American city, individual people and areas live as their own, but each understands their contribution to the grander show. If something can be dreamed of, it can be created here. And if all is possible, there's no need to stress. Chill.

Shot on iPhone 13 Mini

A dream becoming reality is treasure

There's an aliveness here
It's refreshing

Surround our self with those who dream big

Rich Hebron

Talent is the byproduct of practice

Pursuing our dreams is heroic

Our imagination is relentless

Go for it

Be talented
Be professional
Be a fun hang.

The Sun is smiling
Smile back

Being enchanted
silences our doubts

The Sun helps us in immeasurable ways

Why leave a place that provides
every thing we desire?

Our dream is a seed
Nurture it to fruition

How important is quality of life to us?

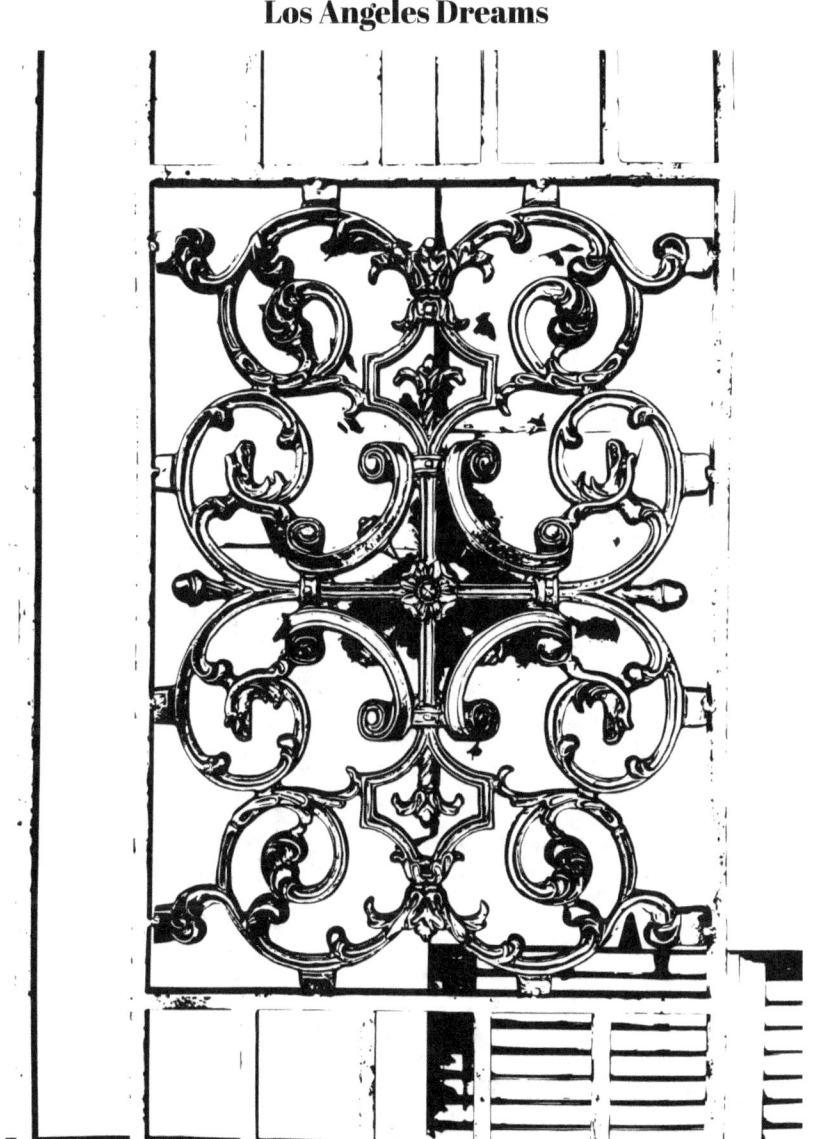

What will we accept?
What will we not accept?
Be vague and specific

Set time aside and focus

What does intuition tell us?

It's easy to love an idea
For it to love us back we must exert effort

Listen to our intuition
We'll know the direction

Pleasant people are delightful

Create what we love
Not what we think others will love

Rich Hebron

Compartmentalize information
What is limited and what is helpful?

Living as dying
Dying as living

People want to come together
It's the cause that's unknown

Vibrant culture leads

Rich Hebron

Why wouldn't we want to be around
people who love us?

Money is just digits

Don't overthink
Decide
Be consistent

We can sense energy

Indulge our curiosity
Ask questions

In the new millennium,
genius is abundance not scarcity

Rich Hebron

Time is wealth

Nothing is precious
except the present
Otherwise life is loss

What do we want?
Lean into our strengths for direction

Strengthen our core so
we don't lean on outside approval

Everything is happening
Do we see it?

Visualize our dream
Believe our dream
Act for our dream

People want to feel good
People want to feel fulfilled
People want to have fun

Break our dream down to its particles
Then assemble the particles into material

Rich Hebron

Believe in our self and fear less

Thinking isn't doing
Doing without thinking is nothing

Rich Hebron

What energizes us today?

Speed of transactions and energy
enable our dreams to blossom

We need more people to
dream with no constraints

Some people don't believe in their dream,
so they believe we can't live our dream

Things are the way they are
because of dreamers
and the lack of dreamers

Dreams used to mean something but,
now, we think we're smarter than our dreams

Listen to every word said
Observe every action

Learn self control and discipline
to realize dreams

The phenomenal is also ordinary

Divine is abundance
Fear is scarcity

Rich Hebron

Understand sources of information

Nothing is sacred
Everything is sacred
Be present and know

Rich Hebron

Be welcome every where

More specific more instruction
More vague more inspiration

Rich Hebron

Is our library of ideas organized?

Fear is the source of suffering

We were told we are phenomenal
because we are phenomenal

The vulnerable receive
more nurture and love

No patting our backs or complaining
will be tolerated

Align our actions with our dream
Move at lightning speed

Rich Hebron

Keep our dream alive
like the flame in our heart

Be where we can breathe
Breathe wherever we be

Rich Hebron

It's like walking through
one large garden of smaller gardens

The Sun is giving and generous of love

Imagine and understand how
today will be fun and like play

We don't have to think
to know the dream inside us

Rich Hebron

The world suffers if we don't live our dream

Give energy and grow regenerative

Rich Hebron

The flowers are never ending and ever living

People want good people to stay

Judging clutters a clear mind

Be clear on how we'll be online

Things are great

Mental and physical
Physical and mental

Do not exert unreasonable effort
Simplicity will suffice

Our mind is a powerful tool

Rich Hebron

Start at the end and work backwards

What if this is easy?

We're into who's into us

A valuable characteristic in a person
is support for our dream and vision

This is going to be fun

Critical thinking and communication
are skills for the future

Rich Hebron

A flexible education is sturdy

Uninspired leads to uninspiring
Uninspiring leads to uninspired

Design and create a sustainable process

Worry leads to things to worry about

Rich Hebron

Understand capabilities of the mind

Reimagine our life
Reimagine our world

What do we see?
What do we think?
How will we move?

Intentional solitude is gold

We can make today whatever we want

Keep moving forward
It may be little but not insignificant

Rich Hebron

Don't paint actions
with a palette of negativity

How available and durable are we?

Don't say yes to things we really mean no to

Be here and now

The dream may be all around us
if we get out of our head

Thoughts can reverberate
through the body and create their selves

Do something not done before

Whatever we think, we're right

Purpose increases life's meaning and joy

Instead of anger, practice patience

The difference between speed and velocity is
that velocity is speed in a direction

Be willing to learn to realize our dreams

Rich Hebron

What patterns do we keep seeing?

What advice would we give our self?

Just figure it out

Worry less about answers
Focus more on questions

Rich Hebron

Do not allow our light to be dimmed
Create a different path and shine bright

A great attitude prevents and solves problems

Have we looked around?
Every thing is working for us

If we don't book it, we won't go

It can be a great day

Shine bright baby

Rich Hebron

The world welcomes us
We've been expected
Now be

Excel with greater
infrastructure and accountability

Approach each conversation
with childlike curiosity

If we cling to our self, we won't learn

Rich Hebron

What do we look forward to?
Forge momentum

Not asked, not getting

Find opportunity in every situation

How does it feel
when the sun kisses our face?

Take a hot bath and relax

Inspire the Divine

Can we see beauty in every thing?

Our rocketship is ready
Blast off to our dreams

A Thought on Cities

Our cities are our greatest invention. They're the engines of civilization. Cities are the hubs that bring people, ideas, and opportunities together. They generate energy and inspire the pursuit of dreams and a better life.

I feel humans are meant to be isolated in nature or surrounded by other humans. Fusing the two maximizes energy and accelerates regenerative processes. This is why I shuffle between living on a farm in rural America and traveling to big international cities.

Having lived in Chicago for over 15 years, I am an enthusiastic advocate for urban living. I believe that the healthier the city, the more dynamic the society and culture. I'm passionate about exploring and analyzing the facets of each city. I believe in competition and that our cities should be constantly learning, adapting, evolving, and growing to serve and increase the quality of life for its residents. I love observing and comparing cities, noting their strengths and weaknesses, the effects of local geography, the movements and flows, and how every small matter contributes to the larger matter.

Cities are where big things happen. I believed this as a little kid growing up on a farm and I know it now as an adult who has experienced their impact.

I'm proud to combine notes that can help realize individual human potential with artwork that demonstrates the beauty collaboration can produce.

Rich leads weekly self-reflection sessions
to help people live aligned with their dreams

Join in on the Rich Conversations Podcast
or visit the Rich Hebron YouTube channel

Connect with Rich: @richhebron

Notes

Notes

Notes

Notes

www.ingramcontent.com/pod-product-compliance
Lightning Source LLC
Chambersburg PA
CBHW071758120626
46550CB00002B/833